40 YEARS IN THE WILDERNESS

**Exodus 14—26; Numbers 14;
Deuteronomy 34:1–6; Joshua 1:9**

Written by Doris Brueggemann
Illustrated by Arthur Kirchhoff

ARCH® Books
Copyright © 1988 CONCORDIA PUBLISHING HOUSE
3558 S. JEFFERSON AVENUE, ST. LOUIS, MO 63118-3968
MANUFACTURED IN THE UNITED STATES OF AMERICA

S0-CMR-582

When Israel fled from Egypt's shores,
The Red Sea waters rose;
Then safely on the other side
They watched the waters close.

"The Lord's strong hand has saved us all,"
Sang Israel that day,
While families with their flocks and herds
Went safely on their way.

Now Moses was their leader, and
Their guide was God the Lord,
Who promised them their own good land—
"Just follow at My word."

They walked through desert wilderness
With watering places few.
"Our children and our cattle thirst!
O God, what shall we do?"

The Lord told Moses, "Take your rod
And strike that rock. Trust Me!"
Then precious water, clear and cold,
Streamed out for all to see.

The food from God for Israel
To gather day and night
Was manna in the morning dawn
And quail in ev'ning's light.

His Ten Commandments God then gave
To guide them every day.
"Now you and all your children learn
To follow and obey."

The Tabernacle was their church,
Where they would hear God's Word.
With silver trumpets, priests would call
To worship God, their Lord.

The only life the children knew
In sunshine and in rain
Was pitching tents and packing up
And wandering again.

But soon they tired of wandering
And fighting nomad bands
Like Moab, Edom, Amalek,
When trav'ling through their lands.

The people grumbled and complained—
Forgot God's love and care!

But Moses begged, "Forgive them, Lord!"
Said God, "I'll grant your prayer."

For 40 years they wandered far,
And older people died;
But Israel grew a nation strong
While trav'ling far and wide.

They dreamed about God's promise that
Beyond the desert sand
It would be green and beautiful—
And *theirs:* The Promised Land!

One hundred twenty years of age
Was Moses, tired and old.
"Another man will lead My people,"
he by God was told.

The Lord chose Joshua, for he
Served God with all his heart;
And Moses blessed him gladly then,
For they were soon to part.

"Our God is with you!" Moses said.
And God blessed Joshua too:
"Be strong, courageous, for I go
With you in all you do."

From high Mount Nebo Moses saw
The Promised Land below.
And then he died. God buried him
Where no one else would know.

We, too, can sing like Israel,
"God is my strength, my Lord!
He leads me in His steadfast love
And guides me with His Word."

DEAR PARENTS:

The story of Israel in the wilderness is a marvelous illustration of God's protection and care for His children and His great patience with them—in spite of enemies, harsh conditions, and their grumbling and ingratitude.

And yet this story is much more than this. We see its full dimensions only in the light of the New Testament. From that vantage point we can observe the full sweep of salvation history—how God chose a people from whom the Messiah would come, how He brought them to the Promised Land, and how He preserved them there until Jesus, the promised Messiah, came to die and rise again for the sins of the world.

Talk to your child about both of these aspects of the story. Our heavenly Father, who protects us and provides all we need, is the same God who in His great love sent Jesus to be our Savior from sin, so that we can live with Him forever in heaven. These indeed are precious truths!

THE EDITOR